BENTLEY AND BLUEBERRY

by Randy Houk

To Dave, and to my mother,
dog lover of all dog lovers.

*O*ne cold day when snow was snowing,
Crusty drifts were slowly growing
Round a kennel, where inside,
Nine new bearded collies cried.

They grew fatter, they grew quickly.
One was big and brown and wiggly,
And the owner's daughter gently
Picked him up, and named him Bentley.

Bentley was just nine weeks old
When Ms. Moody, so I'm told,
Standing by the puppies' pen,
Watched, and saw, and fell for Ben.

She picked him up, she tickled his toes.
Bentley kissed her on the nose.
"Want to go in the 'car-car,' pup?"
She said, and Bentley's eyes said, "Yup!"

3

$\mathcal{B}$entley didn't like the motion,
Like a boat, upon an ocean.
First, he dribbled and threw up.
But he *loved* the car as he grew up.

He rode along wherever it went,
Pushing his nose out the window vent.
Often they drove to a little park,
Where Ben could run, till it got dark.

6

$\mathcal{N}$ear the park, there was another
Scrawny, bearded collie mother,
Trying to keep her litter warm,
Amid a howling winter storm.

In the wind, the puppies quivered,
The puppies shook, the puppies shivered.
Snow blew right into their crate.
They seldom nursed. They seldom ate.

Still, they somehow kept on going,
Though all winter, it kept snowing.
They found scraps and wolfed them down,
From the garbage cans in town.

One pup turned a lovely blue
Shade of gray as up she grew.
She had fleas and she was mangy,
Tall and thin and rough and rangy.

She had ears all full of mites,
Skin infections, from flea bites.
She never heard a van draw near,
She never heard a man say, "Here.

"Come along. We'll fix you up.
You need some help, you poor old pup.
The shelter's got a lovely vet.
She'll fix those fleas and mites, I bet."

The gray was hungry, and alone.
Perhaps he had a scrap, or bone?
Perhaps the man would take her in?
Quietly she went with him.

*M*eanwhile Bentley went to school.
Bentley was nobody's fool.
He'd learn something new each day.
He would heel, and sit, and stay.

Bentley had a braided tug.
He dragged it all around the rug.
With tug in mouth, his eyes would say,
"Ms. Moody, won't you *please* come play?"

$\mathcal{B}$entley had a big ball too.
He could bat it back to you.
Bounce it down the stairs and then,
Fetch, and bounce it down again.

*I*n her cage, the gray dog waits,
And wonders what's outside the gates.
She has no ball, but she has no mites.
She's clean, and fed, and *never* bites.

The warden brings some people by.
"Please pick me," say the gray's sad eyes.
The people choose a golden pup.
The gray stops even getting up.

The warden says, "Sorry. I guess that's that.
There are too many dogs. Too many cats."
He sighs. "A miracle is due.
Somewhere there's a home for you."

$\mathcal{B}$entley is waiting impatiently too.
Something bad happened. Something new.
Ms. Moody has been gone all day.
She has a job. There's no one to play.

Bentley grows desperate and broody.
"*Bentley. Oh,* BENTLEY!" cries Ms. Moody,
Seeing he's eaten a table leg.
"I'm sorry.   Forgive me?" his sad eyes beg.

"This job's *important*," she says then.
"I'm important *too*," thinks Ben.
"I can't just sit and watch the door.
Watching the door is a terrible bore."

"I know what we'll do," she shouts.
"I know how we'll work this out.
Since my dog gets bored alone,
I'll get my dog a dog of his own."

Off they drive, to the local pound.
The warden shows her all around.
"15 million strays a year?"
She says. "Why, I had no idea."

In her cage, the gray hears sounds.
Up her ears go – up she bounds.
Might this be her lucky day?
Might that voice take her away?

She begins a sort of howl,
Not a bark, not quite a growl –
More a kind of whining plea.
"Please," it says. "Oh please pick me?"

"What on earth can that noise be?"
Asks Ms. Moody. "Follow me,"
The warden says. "I think I know."
And off they go – to the very last row.

"*Look*," Ms. Moody says. "My golly.
Surely that's a bearded collie?
She's so droopy.   Is she moping?"
Says the warden, "She's stopped hoping.

"She was ill when she was found.
She's been ten months in the pound.
She spent so much time alone,
She gave up on going home.

"She'll need tags, at little cost,
So you'll find her if she's lost.
She can't have pups, don't be afraid –
All our female dogs are spayed."

"Let's see how the dogs relate,"
Ms. Moody says, and lifts the gate
For the gray, who shakes with joy.
Someone's here for her! *Oh boy!*

Outside, Bentley wags his rear.
He likes this gray.   He makes it clear.
"Well," Ms. Moody says, "I guess –
Bentley says the answer's yes!"

$\mathcal{B}$oth dogs piled into the car.
Home they went. It wasn't far.
Bentley liked this new dog fine,
But he told her, "This ball's *mine!*"

This was not a troubling rule.
The gray was smiling like a fool.
She stood over Ben all day,
So he wouldn't get away.

"Now," Ms. Moody said, "I wonder
Just what name you should go under.
You're a lovely, soft gray-blue –
Blueberry. That's what we'll call you."

Blueberry smiled, then made a puddle.
"*No!* For shame! Oh, what a muddle,"
Said Ms. Moody, frowning sadly.
Blueberry felt very badly.

"I was sure you'd be house-trained.
My poor floor. Oh, what a pain."
Now Blueberry felt afraid.
She began to 'serenade.'

She barked hour after hour.
She barked with increasing power.
"*No!*" Ms. Moody said, "Don't bark."
Blueberry barked till it got dark.

So Ms. Moody called the shelter.
"This dog's barking. Should I belt her?"
"No," the warden said. "Use love.
She'll learn best with a kid glove.

"Don't get mad, don't ever hit 'em.
Those who do, may just get bitten.
You get mad – and so will they.
Teach her. Give her praise each day.

"First, a can of pennies make.
When she barks, give that a shake.
That loud noise will rattle her.
You won't have to battle her."

25

*O*ne day soon, the wood floor glistened.
"Good," Ms. Moody said. Blue listened.
"Good Blue. See that *good* clean floor?"
Soon the puddles were no more.

Ben taught Blueberry how to tug.
They would tug on the living room rug.
Ben taught Blue to fetch the ball,
When he bounced it down the hall.

*I*f you think you want a pet,
And don't care what breed you get,
Go look at the pound's selection –
Strays will give you such affection.

Ben and Blue live happily after,
Filling Ms. Moody's life with laughter.
They live near the Connecticut shore.
And, for now, there is no more.

31

Glossary

kennel	a place where purebred puppies are raised and sold or a place to board pets
bearded collie	a large sheepdog with long hair
motion	movement
scrawny	very thin
litter	all the baby animals born to one mother at the same time
quiver	shake
mangy	covered with sores and skin infections
rangy	long-legged and thin
mites	little bugs that bother dogs and cats
heel	follow close behind
golden	golden retriever, a large, golden haired dog
miracle	a wonderful happening that no one can explain
desperate	almost beyond hope, frantic
broody	thoughtful and sad
strays	dogs and cats that have been lost or have no homes
moping	feeling down and sad
tags	license or i.d. for dogs, with the owner's name and address
spay	an operation on a female dog by a vet (animal doctor) to prevent puppies (male dogs can also be neutered)
serenade	sing loudly
glisten	shine brightly

The real Bentley and Blueberry

The Humane Society of the U.S., a nonprofit organization founded in 1954, and with a constituency of over a million and a half persons, is dedicated to speaking for animals, who cannot speak for themselves. The HSUS is devoted to making the world safe for animals through legal, educational, legislative and investigative means. The HSUS believes that humans have a moral obligation to protect other species with which we share the Earth. For information on The HSUS, call: 202 452-1100.

Text and Illustrations Copyright © 1993 by Randy Houk

Printed by Allied Printing Services
Designed by Anita Soos Design, Inc.

Published by The Benefactory, Inc.
One Post Road, Fairfield, CT 06430
The Benefactory produces books, tapes, and toys that foster animal protection and environmental preservation. Call: 203-255-7744

10 9 8 7 6 5 4 3 2 1

ISBN 1-882728-31-9
Printed in the U.S.A.

THE BENEFACTORY